THE DAWN OF DEBIT CARDS

Jim Beitel

Contents

Foreword ... 1

The Dawn ... 3

The Thrift Industry ... 5

Supermarkets and S&Ls? ... 9

Background ... 11

Interest-ing Innovation ... 15

Lending Innovations ... 19

Tran$matic® ... 21

Plastic Card Accounts—the Un-Passbook ... 25

Going Online ... 31

The IBM 2730 and Supporting Systems ... 35

The Magnetic Striped Card ... 45

The Seeds of Online Electronic Funds Transfers ... 49

Tran$matic® Money Service ... 59

Keeping Things Legal ... 65

We Ramp Up and the Bankers Strike Back ... 69

More Technology	75
TMS Corporation	79
More Innovations	83
Into the NETS Fold	89
Into the Sunset...	93
APPENDIX I - LB269	97
APPENDIX II - 1975 Nebraska Supreme Court Decision	105
About the Author	113

Copyright © 2020 Jim Beitel

All rights reserved.

ISBN: 9798652116798

Dedication

Dedicated to all former employees of First Federal Savings & Loan Association of Lincoln during the 1970s, whose hard work, enthusiasm, teamwork and loyalty made the events described here possible.

Acknowledgements

Like most corporate deeds, this was a team effort. While I'd like to think my contributions to this effort were noteworthy and important, they were certainly no more noteworthy or important than those made by many other players in this story. I will point out a few of the folks as their contributions are related in the story; after all, this is a historically important period within the finance industry.

Also, I will be injecting a few personal anecdotes along the way. These times were, for me, enormously gratifying, and just plain fun. I could hardly believe I was getting paid to be involved with this effort and other enthusiastic people.

Unfortunately, I cannot mention everyone's contributions. They are, in fact, appreciated, and rather than risk leaving out someone, I choose to focus on the key events I can recall and try for the bigger picture. And there is the problem that time has blurred many details in my recollection. Still, I imagine anyone involved would be delighted that this story is being retold now.

Photographs in this publication were obtained from promotional materials created by First Federal Lincoln, IBM and AT&T. As such, they are not covered by this publication's copyright. Images of sample plastic cards were scanned from my personal collection, and likewise are not subject to copyright.

Cover photo credit: IBM.

Foreword

The Dawn of Debit Cards is a first-person recollection of the creation of the world's first debit card-driven electronic funds transfer system; how it came about, how it was received, insights regarding how innovation can happen in unlikely places, and a few personal anecdotes.

Not a lot of information remains available regarding this milestone. Just a couple of archived legal journals refer to proceedings involving this innovation, but lack much context from those involved. Other references to the event contained in publications aiming at a broader context tend to be quite shallow if not downright inaccurate.

This book attempts to fill in much of this context. Technology buffs should be amused as the systems of the day are described.

Bottom line: this book aims to satisfy curiosity regarding how debit cards got started, with historical context and a bit of a humorous perspective.

In addition, this story is a perfect illustration of how a business can use information technology strategically. Because, quite simply, without information technology there would be no debit cards.

The Dawn

Cue music:

Also Sprach Zarathustra, Op. 30, which is better known as the *2001: A Space Odyssey* theme.

Action:

In January of 1974, the president of a rather small financial institution stepped up to the customer service counter in a particular grocery store. He filled out a withdrawal ticket, which at the time included his Personal Identification Number, or PIN (security was not yet a hot button), and presented his magnetic-striped plastic card, and moments later, the first-ever transaction whereby a financial institution account holder was able to withdraw money from their account at the point of sale was history.

Hold that last organ note and... cut!

Okay, maybe this scenario doesn't fill you

with anticipation or excitement. Today, you do it without thinking about it. At the grocery store, hardware store, and gas station—almost everywhere you buy something. You pull out your debit/ATM card, swipe it or insert it and voila! Your transaction is done.

Behind the scenes, somehow the merchant receives money directly from your checking or savings account represented by that debit card you used. This is an example of Electronic Funds Transfer.

This is not the stuff of legends. However, things leading up to the inaugural transaction, and things that transpired in the days, months and years following the event do hold some measure of importance. At least they do for me. I had the exceedingly good fortune to be a part of efforts that brought about this slice of history.

The Thrift Industry

Of some significance, the financial institution in question was not a bank; it was a Savings and Loan association. Collectively known as the thrift industry, S&Ls could not offer checking accounts at that time, and were thus shut out of the normal flow of point-of-sale transactions. If you wanted access to your money, S&Ls had passbook accounts just for you. What's a passbook, you ask?

Simply put, a passbook was a transaction ledger you carried around like a checkbook. Unlike a checkbook, you had to visit your financial institution in order to withdraw or deposit money to this account. Also unlike a checking account, they paid interest.

In most industries, online processing was just taking those first uncertain steps, and the financial industry within which I worked was no exception.

Banking technology gurus of the day were raving about new passbook posting terminals, notably the Burroughs® TC700. These huge things would relieve the teller of having to manually write transactions in their customers' passbooks. Instead, they would (gasp) automatically print them.

Of course, any existing banking software would need some major work in order to do this, including keeping track of which line and page of the passbook was last written on. And this meant you had to be online to the account in question in order for this to work.

This is an example of what is called 'paving a cow path'—speeding up an existing process but doing nothing to re-think those processes.

Magnetic-striped cards had appeared a few years earlier. Invented by IBM®, they were originally used as badge access cards. IBM also sold the 2730 Transaction Validation Terminal, which could read these cards. Gas companies, BankAmericard® (which would become VISA® in 1976), MasterCard® and a host of other private label credit card businesses saw the potential of machine-readable cards in the soon-to-explode online environment.

We saw something else.

The Dawn of Debit Cards

Supermarkets and S&Ls?

Photo Credit: IBM

Pork Chops for 69 cents! A pizza for 59 cents...

Photo Credit: IBM

You might be surprised to learn this history occurred in, of all places, Nebraska. Perhaps even more surprising, it involved a Savings and Loan Association (First Federal Lincoln, short for First Federal Savings & Loan Association of Lincoln, NE; further shorted herein as FFL) and some Hinky Dinky grocery stores.

To the untrained eye, Savings & Loan associations and grocery stores do not exactly suggest hotbeds of innovation.

You would have been wrong to overlook us, though.

Background

For background, we need to look at the banking and thrift arenas in Nebraska in the early '70s. Financial institution activities are regulated, and what follows is an oversimplification, but should serve the purposes herein.

Financial institutions are formed using a structure known as a 'charter'. A charter may be either national or state based.

In Nebraska, the Federal Deposit Insurance Corporation (FDIC) insures the deposits of either national- or state-chartered banks. In the case of state-chartered banks, the FDIC is the primary regulator, while the Office of the Controller of the Currency (OCC) regulates the national banks, although the FDIC has some say in the matter.

Thrift deposits were insured by the Federal Savings and Loan Insurance Corporation

(FSLIC), and the Federal Home Loan Bank Board (FHLBB) regulated S&Ls with this insurance. State charters are not important to this story, so we'll skip their case.

In the time frame we are reviewing—the early 1970s—Nebraska's state banks were not allowed to have branch offices, other than a remote drive-up facility. Because of the MacFadden Act, neither could national banks. So, there were quite a few more banks in that era, because as a customer, you probably picked a bank based on your convenience.

Unlike banks, S&Ls could establish branch offices. But a tightly regulated product line that really could not compete with what banks had to offer offset this competitive advantage.

Automated Teller Machines (ATMs) had been invented, but in use only by larger banks on the coasts whom were implementing online systems. Even so, some Nebraska banks were planning to put ATMs in their locations. The idea of an ATM on every corner hadn't gotten any traction as yet, probably because these early devices were prohibitively expensive.

Financial institutions are nothing if not

The Dawn of Debit Cards

laser-focused on costs. *In-house* automated tellers did make some sense from a cost standpoint. Plus as salesmen would say, they don't get sick, don't go on maternity leave, etc. I doubt this is part of the contemporary ATM sales pitch.

A key element of this story was that in FFLs case, we were under the jurisdiction of the FHLBB, and not subject to Nebraska banking laws. Incidentally, First Federal Lincoln was among the first savings and loans to receive a federal charter and insurance of accounts.

At that time, banks and thrifts were quite different. For the most part, they didn't regard each other as competitors. Banks were where you went for consumer loans, credit cards and checking accounts. Thrifts were where you went for a mortgage to buy your house, or open a Certificate of Deposit or a passbook account. For both banks and thrifts, 'Regulation Q' capped interest rates. Banks could not pay interest on checking deposits. Thrifts were granted a 0.25% higher cap for each rate on other deposit accounts, to help them attract funds to lend.

About the only significant thing an individual S&L could decide regarding interest rates was the interest payment frequency and the compounding interval. Normally, this was pretty much related to the term of the deposit.

Interest-ing Innovation

What the astute customer cared about was the actual yield; that is, the total amount of interest earned as a percent of the balance. The shorter the compounding interval, the higher the yield will be, all other factors being equal.

First Federal Lincoln saw another compounding option: we were the first financial institution to offer 'Continuous Compounding'. On all deposit accounts, certificates included, this allowed us to pay an actual rate slightly more than the competition. We paid the absolute highest yield. Since the compounding interval was up to us, we simply shrugged and chose 'continuous'.

A lot of folks were not too happy about this. I don't remember whom, but some group engaged Harvard University to come out and declare our method invalid. Instead, they did the opposite, which any mathematician familiar with exponentials would readily endorse. Provided, however, that all transactions are assumed to be applied at the end of a business day, which of course they were before real-time online processing got going. Even today, many systems treat real-time balances as 'memo balances', with the actual balance affected at the end of the business day.

Oddly, monthly interest payments were not common; quarterly payments were the norm. The following advertisement from this era shows yet another example of FFLs willingness to innovate:

The Dawn of Debit Cards

Photo Credit: FFL

It didn't take too long for the competition to figure this stuff out and match up. Once interest rates were de-regulated (in 1980), all the compounding hype disappeared, including 'Continuous Compounding'.

Another wrinkle were Split Rate accounts. FFL didn't come up with this idea, but offered such accounts where larger average balances would earn a higher rate.

Lending Innovations

On the lending side of the ledger, First Federal Lincoln was one of the first in Nebraska to offer FHA and VA home loans in the post-war years. FFL continued the innovation, offering something called the 'Savings Mortgage'. You probably know that a mortgage payment usually consists of a Principal amount, an Interest amount, and escrow, insurance and perhaps other amounts.

With the Savings Mortgage, all payments to Principal were accumulated in a 'Savings Fund' balance. You could withdraw and deposit funds to this balance at any time. On a normal loan, the principal balance is paid down gradually over time. In the early payments, very small amounts are applied to principal and thus, larger amounts are collected as interest. This is the result of the process known as 'amortization'.

With the Savings Mortgage, if you added the principal balance and the savings fund balance, you would get the original loan amount. And, when you withdrew from the savings fund, the amount was deducted from the savings fund balance and added back to the principal balance. Conversely, an amount deposited to the savings fund balance was deducted from the principal balance.

This was the forerunner of Home Equity loans, but without the extra paperwork to open such an account. Down the road a few years, FFL even made things easier for the customer by issuing a card that would directly access home equity.

But the first truly lasting innovation was…

Tran$matic®

You may not recognize the name 'Tran$matic®'. And yes, the proper spelling used the dollar sign instead of an 's'. You've seen or used what was done. In essence, when you signed up for Tran$matic®, you authorized FFL to write a check for your mortgage payment or periodic savings deposit on your behalf each month.

Today, you see the same thing not only in mortgage loans; also in utility bills, other types of loans, and even for some private label credit accounts.

To establish the Tran$matic® service, you gave FFL a voided check, from which we stored your checking account number and your bank's routing and transit number. Then, on the fifth (or optionally the twentieth) of the month, we fired up what amounted to a Teletype machine with special magnetic ink and a special mechanism that printed the funny character set on the bottom of checks (called MICR encoding). This technology enables banking 'proof and transit' machines to sort the checking deposits and ultimately get the checks to their proper accounts.

In one pass, we created a lot of customer loan payments, which were deposited just as if the customer had written the payment check and sent it to us, or presented it to a teller. So, customers saved a check, an envelope and stamp or a trip to their branch.

So simple that everyone's doing it now. But FFL did it first, in 1968.

The thing was, while Tran$matic® made life easier for customers; it didn't change life much for the financial industry. It did help with money management, knowing a predictable monthly increase in savings, fewer forgotten or incorrect loan payments and reduced costs not having to prepare and mail loan coupon books and notifications.

It might surprise you that for non-banking financial institutions such as ourselves, we actually needed to maintain at least one checking account at a commercial bank! After all, we had to pay our bills, pay interest to customers that wished to receive this via a check, and handle vault cash requirements. For this, we needed to write checks, and banks were the only game in town for that function.

I point this out, because the banking system in this country relies on regional Federal Reserve Banks wherein commercial banks also maintain at least one account. This is what allows deposits made to one bank using a check from another bank to be settled, so that money moves from the federal account upon which the check was written to the federal account of the bank receiving the deposit.

What was needed to truly revolutionize the financial industry was purely electronic funds transfer at the point of sale. Paper checks and their associated processing would not be involved. What was missing was the ability to electronically transfer money between a *customer's* account at a financial institution and a *merchant's* account.

Plastic Card Accounts—the Un-Passbook

FFLs philosophy really did not include the passbook approach, because they offered only interest paid as competition with checks. They would never be able to provide any utility where checks were used; the point of sale. But plastic cards: there was something with potential.

Well before magnetic stripes appeared on the backs of plastic cards, FFL created a sort of 'un-passbook' account for which the only evidence of ownership was a plain (non-magnetic stripe) plastic card.

Most customers were familiar with credit cards. In those days, I felt neglected if a week went by without receiving at least one of the things in the mail (yes, unsolicited) from gas companies and banks.

FFL knew the un-passbook plastic card

was, in fact, a 'debit card'. But at that time, 'debit' seemed to have a negative connotation among the general public. People associated the word with something 'taken away', which was exactly opposite the reality: A credit relationship with a financial institution meant you owed them money; a debit relationship meant they owed you money (your accounts' funds).

So, the term 'debit card' was not used for several years.

Since there was no passbook involved in which to record transactions, FFL did two things. First, transaction registers were supplied for customers who wished to record their transactions a la the passbook. Second, and more importantly, transaction statements were sent to customers listing, of course, the transactions and interest paid.

The statements resembled banks' checking account statements, perhaps intentionally as a harbinger of things to come. But also, they were initially descriptive years before Regulation E (the Electronic Funds Transfer Act of 1978) mandated such things. Since transactions could be done at any FFL branch, the statements also

The Dawn of Debit Cards

provided the transaction location.

FFL wanted to broaden the 'Tran$matic®' brand. Thus, the new plastic card accounts were referred to as 'Tran$matic®' accounts:

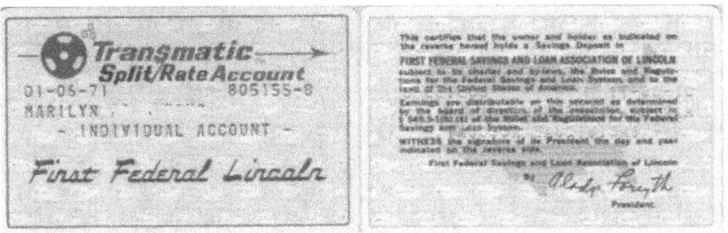

The date opened is embossed rather than an expiration date. So, the embossed data plus the verbiage on the back was almost exactly what would have been printed on a passbook. This kept regulators happy.

This later version was obviously meant to condition customers to the presence of a magnetic stripe even though the fake stripe was blue and on the front of the card! I don't recall if this was a design flaw, or intentional. Note this version used a standard (larger) font for the account number (and the open date, since it was on the same line), which was more closely aligned with credit card standards of the day.

Tran$matic® accounts were classified as 'statement accounts', and the account holders would eventually receive magnetic striped plastics to replace the initial cards issued. Of course that event needed to be coordinated with some sort of ability to actually read the magnetic stripes. That would be accomplished using the IBM 2730 Transaction Validation terminal. Stay tuned for more about that.

A 'Zip-Zap' machine was used to transfer the embossed information on the customer's card, as well as other transaction information such as the date, the branch and teller onto a transaction ticket. At the close of a business day (usually around 4:00 PM), these transaction tickets were forwarded to the Keypunching department, where a group of keypunch operators transcribed the tickets onto IBM cards, so that the transactions could be posted to the proper accounts.

The Dawn of Debit Cards

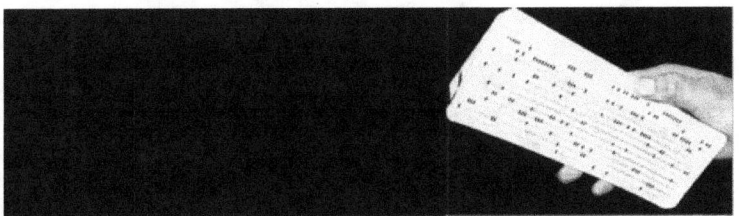

Photo Credit: IBM

The potential for online processing systems to eliminate these sorts of costs were certainly one of the motivations behind FFLs push in that direction.

Going Online

First Federal Lincoln (originally founded as Fidelity Savings & Loan by W. A. Forsyth and eight other men, later managed by Evald Forsyth and upon his death, his wife Gladys Forsyth) was not a large financial institution by any means in the early '70s. Deposits were around 250 million dollars, and soon after I joined the company, the seventh branch opened in Kearney, NE. There were three branches each in Lincoln and Omaha.

In early 1971, I interviewed for a programming job at FFL. Following that, I (stupidly, I suppose) told a friend, Ike Schneider, about the job. Guess who got hired? Luckily we were good enough friends that he lobbied for hiring me as a night computer operator a few weeks later, just to get me on the team. It wasn't long before I started programming in addition to still operating the computer and going to school.

We were a great team; both of us saw

things the other had missed; yet we usually had exactly the same mental picture of what we were trying to accomplish. We were both studying Computer Science at the University of Nebraska, and were working together on a class project which involved writing, of all things, an online banking system.

FFL had recently acquired a (really, really) small IBM System/360 Model 25 computer, with 64Kbytes of memory. Not Gigabytes. Not Megabytes. 65,536 total actual bytes. Unbelievable to think about now: my iPhone is 32 Gigabytes and millions of times faster.

IBM was attempting to write the underpinnings for an online system for FFL. Products like CICS (Customer Information Control System) did not yet exist, although it was coming to market within the year. CICS provides the framework to develop online systems; called a 'Teleprocessing Monitor' system in those days.

The reasons IBM was contracted to develop the initial online system for FFL were two-fold:

1. No existing software was available

to support the 2730 terminals on small systems such as FFLs, including the anticipated CICS;

2. When the contract was negotiated, FFLs small programming staff (who didn't include Ike or myself) was not capable of doing this kind of programming without significant investments of time and money in education. Their plates were full trying to keep an old pre-System/360 system running.

FFL strategy with respect to information technology was beginning to emerge. Magnetic striped cards were in existence, and the IBM 2730 device was an inexpensive means to support them. Connecting the dots, when information technology can capture the plastic card account information, then an online system can eliminate keypunching, and for that matter, the entire manner of processing transactions. They allow real-time account balances, which are mandatory for debit cards to be viable.

In contrast, credit card processing in this time frame didn't much care about your balance. If you exceeded your credit limit, the credit card company would send you a nasty letter, and provide a list of over-limit customer numbers to vendors, ostensibly to prevent further transactions. Individual vendors would swallow any major over-limit transactions, so it was in their interest to review this list as part of the transaction process.

Clearly, this situation would be obsolete sooner rather than later, but it would require online transaction processing to facilitate the desired situation.

The IBM 2730 and Supporting Systems

You might wonder why I want to go into some detail about the initial hardware and software. Simple: This was the configuration that was used to make history. And at no additional cost, you might get a chuckle or two. That said, I won't mind if you skip ahead…

The 2730 was a pretty simple device about half the size of a typewriter, consisting of a 12-key numeric and functional keyboard, a slot to hold the customer's magnetic striped card, and another one to hold the terminal operator identification card, a mechanism to allow a read head to read the magnetic stripes, and an acoustical coupler for connection with a standard telephone handset.

The following picture (as well as the cover photo) was taken in our home office, and was used in an IBM publication called an

'Application Brief' from March 1975: **No-Passbook Transactions Using Magnetic Stripe Cards and the IBM 2730**. Catchy title. Sums things up nicely. The booklet featured the FFL system at that time.

Photo Credit: IBM

Tellers would call the FLL computer line, which would answer the calls using an IBM 7770 Audio Response Unit (a refrigerator-sized box), which in turn was attached to the computer. The computer would cause the 7770 to speak a greeting (in our case, it would say "Proceed.")

Input was done using a simple data transmission technology similar to what is used for Fax. The data is transmitted using sound, which is why the 2730 telephone interface is called an acoustic coupler. The coupler fit over the telephone mouthpiece (in the previous picture, it's black on the white phone. This transmission technology is known as Frequency Shift Keying (FSK), in case you're wondering.

Output, as already indicated, was spoken words. The 7770 could carry on eight conversations at a time, which sounds a bit underwhelming. Still, busy signals were extremely rare, even in peak periods.

This is getting ahead of the story, but here's how a transaction (e.g. withdrawal) would be processed. After dialing the computer's phone number and hearing the greeting, the teller would key in a code indicating 'withdrawal', the amount, and the customer's PIN. Then, she would draw a spring-loaded mechanism across the magnetic striped cards loaded into their trays and release the bar. This caused the magnetic stripes to be read and transmitted.

Once the computer received this message, the 'app' to process the withdrawal was loaded, and all the necessary changes to files were made to create the withdrawal transaction in the system. Then, the program would compose a response (using a string of numbers corresponding to the available vocabulary words in the 7770) that might result in something like "Account eight zero zero one type eight zero withdrawal two five dollars zero zero cents..." and so on.

The teller could choose to accept or cancel this entry by entering the appropriate code.

Q: Why was this particular equipment being used?

A: Because it was literally the only available low-cost way to process transactions using magnetic striped cards in the IBM world, which included FFL.

Think about this: phone companies primarily used audio response systems at this time. It's a stretch to be able to see them as online transaction processing systems. Yet that was exactly what IBM had in mind for this equipment, and found a willing partner in FFL.

The first 'swipe reader' wouldn't be available for at least four more years. In

The Dawn of Debit Cards

addition, typewriter-like terminals were to be deployed for situations requiring printed output or longer responses than would be practical using audio responses. In the home office where the computer was located, IBM 2260 CRTs would also be used, primarily for back-office information look-up and data entry. These would soon be replaced with new 3270 technology, whose protocol is still the standard today for mainframe terminal communications.

Back to the story, wherein IBM was programming the initial online system for FFL... Ike and I convinced FFL to cut IBMs effort short and let us apply what we had already done in school. Ike handled much of the programming for what our tellers and other users would be doing online (today those would be 'apps'). Along with our boss and other programming staff, he also took care of the batch processing systems wherein most of the accounting and account processing was performed. That was programmed using COBOL. I tackled the infrastructure for the online system using Basic Assembler Language (BAL). We all shared in design, which was done almost daily, on the fly.

We were supposed to reuse as much of the

IBM prototype as we could. After all, FFL had paid some serious money to have it done. We were able to salvage a lot of the 'apps', but the infrastructure was another matter; it was absolutely not scalable software.

Meaning, as more users added more volume, the only way to handle it would have been to buy ever-larger computers. Saaay... I wonder if this had occurred to IBM... So, most of this programming code turned into 'comments' (meaning they were printed along with actual programming code but played no role beyond that), and disappeared altogether as soon as it was feasible.

What was needed to make the system do more with limited resources (be scalable) is way, way beyond the scope of this story. Suffice it to say that's why people study Computer Science in college. Nevertheless, the initial 'toy' computer (IBM/360 Model 25) was seriously undersized and lasted less than a year before making way for an IBM/370 Model 135.

I had a reputation of getting my programs to run—correctly—on the first try. Would this include the rewrite of IBMs prototype of our online system? This was a system which managed communications with terminal devices and managed file access on behalf of 'application programs' written in COBOL that were invoked by whatever codes the users supplied through their terminals. It was not a simple undertaking.

Compounding the hurdle was the fact that at that point in time, programs were input to the computer using punched cards, along with daily transaction input as previously noted. Yes, one programming line per card at a time.

As I write this now on my laptop, I recall how laborious it was to fix keypunching errors. First, you listed the card deck on a printout. Then you examined the programs with a fine-tooth comb. Then you punched the corrected cards and replaced the bad ones, trying not to drop or otherwise mess up the other cards.

Further compounding the hurdle was FFLs tiny system. The *whole online system*, including all application programs, needed to be shoehorned into 8,192 bytes of memory. That's 8KB, one fourth of the total system memory.

The stack of punched cards that made up this system was fed through a reader to be 'assembled' and made into a program that could be 'executed' (run on the computer; not killed!).

I still recall the people watching the proceedings. I was making beer bets with everyone on the outcome. Step One was to actually create the aforementioned executable program without errors...

Mission accomplished!

Step Two was the actual test: the operator entered the command sequences to execute the system. After this was entered and acknowledged by the operating system, nothing happened. This was a good thing: it meant the system was waiting for terminal input...

Everything worked! I enjoyed collecting those beer bets!

Later, I would very nearly avoid something that would have removed me from being in the thick of things and would have completely changed my life and career. That something was called the military draft. As in being drafted for military service, which at the time was a certain ticket to Vietnam.

My student deferments had finally run out after six years of college. As fate would have it, one week before my induction was to begin, President Nixon announced the end of the draft! Immensely relieved, I continued on, resulting in now being able to relate this little tale.

Ike was taking the ROTC approach. He was married, and with some help from FFL's Executive Vice President was able to defer his tour of duty a couple of years, allowing the team to proceed.

The Magnetic Striped Card

We were able to bring our teller lines in all branches into the online era in a little more than a year. This included the issuing of magnetic striped cards to the transaction account holders.

Since no one had issued magnetic stripe debit cards to their customers before, we needed to come up with the standard for how to encode the magnetic stripe. We wound up re-issuing the plastic cards a few times, once industry standards stabilized. Our initial effort used an emerging standard promoted by the thrift industry. This proved to be either shortsighted or wildly optimistic, or both.

There's a lesson here: "Just do it."

Around this time, the magnetic striped cards used a magnetic stripe wide enough to hold two separate tracks of data. If you could peer into the magnetic structure of these stripes, they would resemble bar codes, such as the UPS code found on nearly everything you can purchase.

Track 1 was reserved for use by the airline industry. Track 2 was for use by the finance industry, and that's where we stored our data. Later, the thrift industry lobbied for, and was granted, additional standards for a track 3. Of course, the original width of the magnetic stripe wouldn't hold another track. And by the time cards began to appear with wider stripes, no one cared to use the thrift standard!

The reason was that another standard emerged from the American Bankers Association (ABA), and if anyone wanted to be able to use any future nationwide network, this standard was the most likely to be required. This format specified Track 2.

Here's the initial magnetic striped card issued to existing transaction account holders and for any new accounts moving forward:

The Dawn of Debit Cards

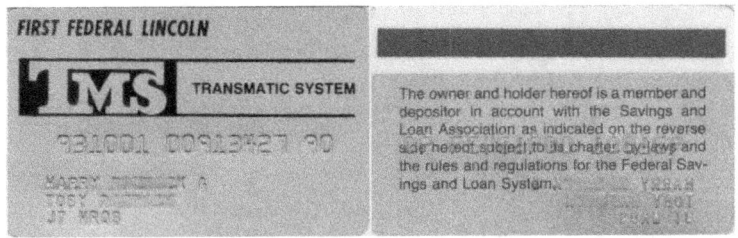

Note that date opened was no longer used, and an institution identifier (S&L standard) was added ('931001' indicated FFL).

There's that tie-in with Tran$matic® again. In fact, TMS would soon represent 'Tran$matic® Money Service.

The Seeds of Online Electronic Funds Transfers

Some of the players in this story other than Ike and I need to be introduced. Earlier I mentioned Gladys Forsyth and her husband, who had passed away years before this story takes place. So it was Gladys who really built First Federal Lincoln, and ran the company for many years. At that point in time this story begins, she was still active as our President and Chairwoman of the board.

Powerful women running anything, let alone an S&L, were rare. But powerful she was; FFL was known as a women's company. She was progressive enough to see the future we all were aiming for, and for the most part, stayed out of the way.

FFL was a very 'parental' organization in those days, in stark contrast to corporate America today. For example, the home office, as well as another office in Omaha ('Homestead') contained cafeterias, and provided free, warm lunches for employees. (They were delivered to other branches.)

Christmas parties were legendary events held at the aforementioned Homestead branch, including a bus from Lincoln so everyone would have an hour to sober up rather than attempting to negotiate the Interstate following the festivities. A highlight was a rendition of *'White Christmas'* by Harry Mickelson. But I digress...

Females held many important management roles, including the emerging data processing organization of which I was a part. Eldon Jameson had done some programming prior to the IBM/360 era, and was the 'Systems Analyst' when I joined. Ike and I reported to him. He later became the Director of Information Services.

Soon after I joined the company, Eldon reported to Lavern (Vern) Roschewski, our treasurer and the unofficial COO of the company. I say that because nothing important happened without Vern's approval. Vern was really the brains behind a lot of the innovation. He was a master at reading and interpreting regulations to suit the desired plans. He seemed to possess the power to make "no" into "yes" at will.

But the guiding force behind our innovation was John E. Dean. (No relation to Nixon's John Dean of Watergate fame.) Mr. Dean was executive vice president, and became the president of FFL in 1974. He was the son-in-law of Gladys Forsyth. John was also an attorney, and his law office was in the building housing the home office.

Mr. Dean was already well known in the thrift industry as the 'father of Tran$matic®'. I assume he was a pretty sharp attorney, having tried and won a Supreme Court case. He was one of those people for whom 'upsetting the applecart' was an imperative.

Photo Credit: FFL

One of the most important lessons I've

taken from this entire experience is the importance of **vision**. John Dean was certainly a visionary. Where others saw a stable (boring), niche thrift industry, Dean saw numerous opportunities to take on the banking industry and beat them at their own game.

Mr. Dean correctly foresaw the coming deregulation of interest rates, and the possibility of branch banking in Nebraska. These would, of course, negate the only leverage a thrift institution had for remaining viable. He often muttered about the huge advantage banks had with 'free money'. He was referring to the fact that thrifts had to pay interest for every deposit, while banks paid nothing for checking deposits. So, he constantly looked for ways to compete with banks, not just other thrifts.

So, this cast of characters (except for Gladys, other than occasionally and usually including a few other managers) would gather after work for a beverage or so nearly every night. I quickly learned that these gatherings were by far the most important time of the day, if you wished to participate in the future of the company.

The Dawn of Debit Cards

For several years, the venue of choice was the legendary Hob Nob bar and grille. This was the typical old establishment with a spectacular wood and marble antique mirrored bar, which was rumored to have come from San Francisco. In addition to the requisite bar stools, there were tables and booths. The food was really pretty good: steaks, burgers, chicken etc. But I digress...

One night in 1973, I was sitting next to Mr. Dean. To review: We had issued magnetic-stripe cards and were utilizing them in our online system via the IBM 2730 terminals to perform teller transactions.

Customers seemed to like this a lot. We had, for all practical purposes, abandoned passbooks.

Mr. Dean drew a stick-person teller and our computer on the back of a cocktail napkin (were else?) and showed it to everyone. He asked how, when a customer withdraws money, were we able to process this online. Of course, he knew, but someone added the data and accounting flow to the napkin.

"Now, what if the teller isn't our employee, but is a merchant employee using our system in a merchant's store" he asked. We thought about it, and quickly realized that our branch settlement (in the General Ledger) could be extended to include merchant 'branches' and 'tellers'. The only addition was a statement account owned by the merchant. There would be additional settlement transactions to this account that weren't necessary for in-house tellers.

For example, a cash withdrawal of $100 at a merchant would actually result in a transfer of $100 from the customer's account to the merchant's account, with the General Ledger reflecting this in the merchant settlement.

All electronic; No paper or checks involved, other than the withdrawal ticket at the point of sale, which served a backup/recovery role. We had just designed the foundation for debit card Electronic Funds Transfer.

It was then I also realized that what we were talking about was no longer limited by geography.

"Let's do it, then."

Mr. Dean was clearly thinking strategically about this. And, clearly, information technology was a key part of the strategy. And hopefully, it is clear that information technology representatives needed to be in the room when strategy was being formed!

FFL didn't have formal strategic planning meetings in these days. In hindsight, the after-hours gatherings often involved strategy formulations. Long before the back-of-the-napkin strategy that opened the door to merchant-operated terminals, important components of strategy were formulated regarding the need for online processing, how to accomplish real-time balances, and many other strategic elements.

As promised, it wasn't difficult to make the leap to a merchant-operated terminal, and provide real-time settlement. Mr. Dean and Mr. Roschewski began lining up Hinky Dinky Supermarkets for a test. They worked with the FHLBB to obtain the necessary permissions and waivers to allow us to proceed.

We gained all sorts of national attention and publicity. Messrs. Dean and Roschewski travelled to various conventions telling various trade gatherings what was coming. Finally, at a meeting in Chicago needed to obtain final approval to launch the 'pilot test', a demonstration was planned.

Here is where I explain how NOT to keep the best job you've ever had.

On the day of the demonstration, I discovered a bug. It could have waited. But my idea was to create a test version with the bug fix, leaving production programs alone.

You already know what happened. The test version somehow became the production version. The bug fix had unintended consequences.

On top of that, Eldon (who was along to set up the demo) wanted to test the system just as the fertilizer was hitting the fan back home. Needless to say, he wasn't overly happy with the proceedings. I calmly told him it would be fixed shortly and to try again in twenty minutes. I was told I had ten before the live demo started—some VIPs couldn't wait for the scheduled demo.

Happily, my fixes worked. I sometimes wonder how my life would have turned out if they hadn't

Tran$matic® Money Service

On January 14, 1974 we went live with the Tran$matic® Money Service in two Hinky Dinky stores. Customers now could deposit or withdraw money here without needing a check; just their Tran$matic® plastic card. Plans to incorporate all the Lincoln and Omaha locations, and other towns in which we had branches were in the works.

To say this idea was popular was an understatement: First Federal Lincoln opened 672 new accounts representing more than $310,000 in new deposits in a matter of days. Existing customers increased their net balances by more than $290,000. This may not sound like a lot these days, but it was astonishing in 1974 for a thrift institution.

One reason Hinky Dinky stores were selected for the pilot was that Cullum Companies of Dallas, DBA American Stores, owned them. Therefore, they would be immune to a lot of political pressure from any Nebraska banks.

And needless to say, Nebraska bankers were less than enthusiastic with our success. Remember: At that time in Nebraska, branch banking was not allowed, so here we were with our growing branch network and soon-to-be merchant network. Also at that time, some banks had ATMs, but they had to be on-premise. That was going to change soon, but we would have a big head start.

Worst of all from the bankers' point of view, *we suddenly were competing on their turf with something that had the obvious potential of eliminating checks*! Indeed, stories extolling the 'checkless-cashless society' were everywhere in the national media. Not to mention the obvious capability to do this anywhere you could find a telephone.

So, the bankers did the only thing they could do to stop us: they sued.

A federal law, known as the MacFadden Act, specifies competitive equality provisions which put federally chartered banks on equal footing with state chartered banks. It basically equally limits these entities to what the various state laws allow.

Since federal savings and loan associations are not subject to these provisions, the state could not directly challenge FFLs EFT system.

Therefore, the state attorney general brought a *quo warranto* (by what authority are you doing this?) proceeding to revoke the charter of the parent corporation of Hinky Dinky, which included a cease and desist until the matter was resolved. The attorney general asserted that our 2730 terminal was really a bank being operated by Hinky Dinky in violation of state banking laws.

He argued that if a bank were to put such a terminal in place and operate it with a bank employee, it would be illegal. He attempted to make the point that merchant operation of the terminal didn't change anything.

The Independent Bankers Association of America joined the suit as *amicus curiae* (friend of the court), arguing that, regardless of the FHLBBs jurisdiction to permit us to engage in EFT systems, the laws of Nebraska prohibit the participation in such arrangements by retail stores licensed to do business in the state.

A Nebraska Supreme Court ruling was required to get us back in business. This event took well over a year, and was delivered on May 1, 1975. The gist of the ruling was:

> The FHLBB has absolute jurisdiction in the matter;

> The FHLBB had granted approval for FFL to undertake the EFT 'pilot test';

> The FHLBB had granted the right for FFL to utilize an agent (merchant employee) to operate the terminal;

> A banker-depositor relationship can only be created by contract, and no new accounts were created with the system;

> So, the debtor-creditor relationship essential to a bank deposit or withdrawal never exists between the customer and Hinky Dinky;

> The funds transfer transactions are carried out on the premises of First Federal Lincoln electronically, so therefore Hinky Dinky is merely acting as a financial and operational

intermediary, not as a bank.

Case dismissed. (See full text of ruling in Appendix II.)

Articles were all over the nationwide press, such as **"Will supermarkets like this become S&L 'branches'?"** Hold that thought for a bit.

Keeping Things Legal

I was not part of any of the testimony regarding the case, but was able to stay abreast of the proceedings via the after-hour gatherings. I learned a very important lesson regarding testimony: Everything said will be taken literally. For example, in the course of testimony, the process of real-time settlement was brought up.

Settlement is the name given to the process of balancing a financial institution's accounting (General Ledger). For example, there might be a General Ledger account for cash, which would be balanced by adjusting the account for the difference between cash deposits and loan payments, and cash withdrawals and other outgoing cash payments. This net difference adjustment is posted to the General Ledger cash account.

Most banking settlement occurs at the close of business, using a minimum of 'net' transactions. We had testified to 'real-time' settlement, but didn't explain the distinction between a real-time 'memo' balance, and the posted balance determined after close of business. So, there was a problem. Because customers could deposit money along with withdrawing it at the merchant locations, the possibility existed for the merchant's transaction (memo) account balance to become negative on a real-time basis.

For example, a customer might deposit proceeds from selling their car, say $5,000. The transaction would add $5,000 to the customer's account and deduct $5,000 from the merchant account. If prior to this, the merchant account's real-time balance was less than $5,000, this transaction would cause a negative real-time balance, and as an S&L, such an occurrence appeared to be illegal. Not wishing to stir up the pot, we needed to be able to testify regarding how this would be handled legally.

The solution defies common sense, but saved the day: We altered the programming to incorporate Tran$matic® transactions! Meaning, the merchant's transaction account balance was checked prior to performing a transaction to determine whether or not there were sufficient funds available.

If not, the rickety old Tran$matic® check printer sprung to life and created the necessary number of (pre-authorized fixed amount) deposit checks drawn on the merchant's bank account required to keep the memo balance positive after the pending EFT transaction. Then, a special 'electronic teller' jumped the line in front of the pending EFT, and a real-time deposit of these items was done to the merchant's transaction account. The result: as testified to, the merchant's account balance was always kept in the black.

After some period of time, this Rube Goldberg setup died a quiet, undocumented death, and settlement occurred at the close of business, as with the rest of the world.

We Ramp Up and the Bankers Strike Back

While things were at a standstill because of the cease and desist, a few of us became writers. Literally, we spent six months documenting in detail how the system worked, how to program new features with the online system, etc. We did this thinking that in order to get other financial institutions to use TMS, they would need to buy our software.

As well as our system functioned, it was, in fact pretty much thrown together over the course of a year or so, and had already become difficult to maintain. It would need a lot of work to become a product.

In addition to the state case, the bankers also tried to get better results in Federal court, but this action did not include additional cease and desist, and also failed.

Meanwhile, the Nebraska bankers became involved in a flurry of activity, perhaps sensing their lawsuits would ultimately be struck down. They established the Nebraska Electronic Transfer System, or NETS for short. They worked hand in hand with the state legislature to draft LB 269. (See Appendix I for the full text.)

LB 269 consisted of three parts: it altered the branch banking section of the Nebraska Banking Act (opening the door for branch approvals down the road, and off-premise facilities immediately), it provided for the computer and communications equipment necessary for electronic funds transfer systems (EFTS) in Nebraska, and it established the methods of operations for EFTS in the state.

Newspaper accounts told of legislators whom urgently advocated passage of LB 269 so that the banking industry "might curb the head start achieved by federal savings and loans and obtain a fair opportunity to compete with such services as First Federal's Tran$matic® Money Service". On May 2, 1975, LB269 passed, and Nebraska became one of a very few states to have EFT law at that time.

The applecart had indeed been upset! John Dean truly wanted to share the TMS terminals with banks, not just other thrifts. But initially, bankers didn't wish to reciprocate.

LB 269 went the distance to help level the playing field among all Nebraska banks with rules regarding sharing, customer access, and so on. However, it pointedly excluded other financial institutions from participation (First Federal Lincoln need not apply.)

NETS-like systems were popping up in many other states around this time. But the NETS network design was unique. Most early networks simply provided a path between banks. Each bank would connect to the 'switch', as the network hub was called.

It was up to the banks to run their own ATMS, keep those transactions which could be handled on their system, and pass along those belonging to some other bank. NETS also provided these paths, but included ATM processing. Lots of small banks liked this idea because they didn't have to invest in processing systems nor pay a correspondent bank to do so. (A 'correspondent bank' is simply a bank that provides servicing to other, smaller banks including check processing, data processing, and etc.)

As we saw it, our approach was better than ATMs, because in those days, it took a large sum of money to install an ATM, while a 2730 was peanuts. Plus, we had the human interaction and ability to manually work around problems. When an ATM was down, you were not getting your money anytime soon. With TMS, unless all the phones were down, you could still get your money.

Being online puts more pressure on operations to ensure the system stays running. With a merchant network involved, the online hours were also longer than simple office hours. We drilled into the computer operators' heads to get help if something happened that they couldn't handle.

One evening a particularly conscientious operator was on duty, and there was some problem causing the system to fail repeatedly. He grew more frustrated as he walked down the list of people to call, coming up with no one home. Of course, we were all at the bar down the street.

Finally, someone's wife told him where everyone was and suggested he simply run over there and get help. By then he was near panic, so he dashed down the street and into the bar where we all were gathered.

Wide-eyed, out of breath, and looking a bit disheveled, he blurted out at a level the whole place could hear: "I CAN'T GET IT UP!"

Crickets. Followed by pandemonium. I never saw a face that red before or since.

More Technology

Somewhere in all of this, we attracted the attention of Bell Labs. Of course, the time frame in question is prior to the breaking up of AT&T. Bell Labs was AT&T's technology group, having invented Unix, the C language and of course the majority of the nation's telecommunications hardware and network.

We got on their radar because they were coming up with something called the 'Transaction Telephone'. Basically, it was a telephone with a magnetic stripe card reader attached. The following shows a historical photo of the Transaction Telephone that appeared in a free poster provided by AT&T, along with an ad promoting the device (finally, a 'swipe' reader!):

Photo Credit: AT&T

Another long story short: we were one of the first to deploy the Transaction Telephone. Bell Labs deployed a team of three engineers to FFL armed with a prototype. It didn't require much effort to support the device, and as I recall, didn't take Bell Labs long to get production devices in our hands. We replaced all the IBM 2730s in short order.

We were working to support it's follow-on, creatively named the Transaction Telephone II, which oddly was not a telephone at all; it used a display rather than audio response. However, this product did provide a PIN Pad, but lacked PIN encryption. So what?

Actually, our initial debit card plans didn't even include a Personal Identification Number (PIN). But before we ever deployed debit cards with a magnetic stripe, we concluded this was a necessity. At a minimum, matching the PIN with the card suggested the cardholder was legitimate. But PIN security wasn't initially a thing.

The first transaction tickets included four large boxes for the customer to write their PIN, so the terminal operator (teller or merchant) could then enter it as part of the transaction. It was unbelievably difficult for customers to remember this PIN! People would write it on the card, or use a 4-digit number they couldn't forget, such as their birthday (mm/dd).

Tellers, always trying to provide great customer service, would remember their good customers' PINs.

As nationwide networks evolved, PIN security started to become more important. For example, ABA magnetic stripe standards began to specify a 'PIN Offset'. Initially, deriving this 4-digit number was up to the card issuer. The idea was that the card issuer's system would validate it. However, some institutions would simply store the PIN as the PIN Offset, which was not secure. Anyone could buy inexpensive stripe readers.

So, version two required a specific algorithm for calculating the Offset, soon also requiring hardware encryption/decryption. Jumping ahead a bit, with the advent of VISA Debit we joined the world of encryption, key management, et al. VISA even provided the VISA Security Module—hardware to perform encryption/decryption.

This type of security depends entirely on preserving the secrecy of a 'Master Key'. The contrast with the clear PIN world with which we began could not be more striking.

Which is why, in the time frame we're reviewing, the Transaction Telephone II was dead on arrival. At least as far as we were concerned.

TMS Corporation

As previously implied, IBM played an important supporting role in all of this. The most significant point of contact between IBM and companies they serve is the IBM Sales Representative assigned to the account. Two such salesmen, John Lydick and George Peterson, filled this role over the time period covered so far in this tale.

As IBM is famous for, these guys worked more with FFL management, and John Dean in particular, than they did with the data processing organization. Mr. Dean discussed his vision of a nationwide TMS system with them many times.

So perhaps not surprisingly, Mr. Dean hired both Mr. Lydick and Mr. Peterson, and spun off TMS Corporation of the Americas to market our idea to other financial institutions. ('TMS Corporation of the Americas" was used because there apparently are many TMS-named companies. While wordy, it was unique.)

In addition, we needed to call what we were doing something other than Tran$matic Money Service, because Mr. Dean had previously sold the name Tran$matic to the U. S. League of Savings Associations for one dollar. (Messrs. Lydick and Peterson wished to aim a bit higher with regard to brand revenue.)

Accordingly, Mr. Lydick hired a noted New York brand strategy firm (Lippincott & Margulies) to come up with a replacement for Tran$matic® Money Service.

This led to the nationwide version of 'the Money Service®' debit card. Graphics in the white space were custom by institution. Note use of an ABA-standard institution identifier. 'Prestige' graphic indicates participation in nationwide emergency cash system. Note also the wider magnetic stripe, which by this time, no one cared about.

Thus 'The Money Service®' was born. The rollout was pretty successful, too. I don't recall the actual number of licensees, but it was sufficient to host annual conferences in places like the Sea Pines Plantation on Hilton Head Island, SC.

A good number of licensees didn't have their own computer software, or systems for that matter, and most were not able to implement the interfaces needed to use the network. Therefore, selling our software wasn't a viable solution. Because of this, we offered account servicing using our system, initially for TMS accounts. It wasn't long before clients were begging for full product servicing, which we were able to provide in a few months' time.

We became something akin to a correspondent bank, although there was never a term applied to non-bank financial institutions.

Interestingly, providing full account servicing didn't require a large increase in our staffing. As I recall, we only added two or three people company-wide to perform this work. This was because we didn't provide any unique features; everyone got the same things.

An aside: We felt this account servicing was a financially positive enterprise. I learned something about politics, though, as it wasn't in the interest of some managers that our operation would show a profit. Therefore, cost accounting studies would somehow show losses.

We even put together a detailed business plan, whereby we would become a subsidy of FFL, like TMS Corporation, returning a minimum of 10% on investment. It should have been a no-brainer. No dice. As I said… politics.

More Innovations

I was not privy to all the proceedings leading up to an agreement with the Omaha National Bank, but the move was pure genius. Omaha National Bank was sort of a 'rogue' bank, always pushing the limits of the law, and upsetting other Nebraska banks for various reasons. So, we were kindred spirits, I suppose.

Under this agreement, ONB could access our entire merchant terminal network and in turn, we could come into NETS through their back door. Bottom line: ONB and FFL customers could use any remote ATM or merchant terminal they wanted to use.

It didn't take long for ATM fees to appear. Perhaps they were coming anyway, but the ONB-FFL agreement certainly seemed to hasten the implementation.

Sadly, as everything was ramping up, Mr. Dean passed away in 1976. As a visionary, a strong advocate of innovation and calculated risk-taking, he was impossible to replace. Slowly but surely, the bean-counter mentality worked its way into the process, and things were never really the same. Still our momentum carried us along for several years to come.

Fortunately, innovation didn't end with Mr. Dean's death:

We were one of the first financial institutions in the nation to offer telephone bill paying. As an S&L, this offering created for our customers another reason not to need a checking account; a simple phone call resulted in causing the bills to be paid, rather than writing and mailing checks. Of course, we were writing the checks, which ironically led us to finally offering a check-like product:

We were the first S&L to offer interest-bearing checking accounts (called, at first, 'NOW accounts'). These things originated in New England savings banks (a slightly different charter than thrifts). We believed the FHLBB regulations allowed us to offer Negotiable Orders of Withdrawal—a fancy term for checks, provided they were drawn on a national bank.

The Dawn of Debit Cards

We were allowed to use such items for bill payments, so we connected the dots, and allowed these to access our transaction accounts, which of course, paid interest.

An aside: These NOWs were drawn on Chase Manhattan Bank, which had been following our story from the beginning. They even sent a team to Lincoln early in the timeline to talk with us and to get a better understanding of what we were doing. They could not believe we were fully online with such a tiny computer system, to the point of trying to get us to divulge the location of the 'real' computer!

Also, we only offered these accounts with truncated checks. In other words, when you wrote a check, a copy was made on 'NCR paper' directly under the item. When this check was deposited, it was filmed and stored ('truncated') at that point, meaning the customer statements never included cancelled checks. This was relatively unique at that time.

We were among the first financial institutions to issue both VISA® Debit and Credit cards. Today, almost all financial institutions issue VISA® (or MasterCard®) Debit cards, rather than or in addition to a network-branded card (e.g. a card which can be used in the NETS world). Obviously, this card would be accepted wherever VISA®/MasterCard® is accepted. And, they would work in virtually all ATM networks.

We originally called these things 'plastic checks'. But I recall some sort of brouhaha over that, and it was later dropped.

Looks like a typical VISA® card, right? Wrong. It's one of the nation's first VISA® Debit card. This sample had not yet been embossed—if it had, it would look similar to any other VISA® card, including (finally) an expiration date. The little logos (called 'bugs') tell the customer which ATMs or POS networks will accept the card. Of course, it can also be used wherever VISA® is accepted. Also note this was the first debit card you actually signed!

The Dawn of Debit Cards

These days, the word 'Debit' must appear on the card. I'm not certain why, since you can easily tell the difference by looking at the back of the card.

The saying, "when the only tool you have is a hammer, everything looks like a nail" seemed to apply to VISA® Debit cards for FFL. Here's one that accessed a home equity line of credit:

Nationally, a competing brand emerged called 'PassCard™'. Clever name that tried to hook the familiar passbook with the new technology. Ultimately, I think people quickly forgot about passbooks—I know our customers certainly did. TMS Corporation eventually acquired PassCard and all their licensees, although no effort was made to eliminate the PassCard name to my knowledge.

Into the NETS Fold

Some time in the mid '80s, First Federal Lincoln officially became a member of NETS. We even were given a seat on the board, including a seat on the executive committee. I know, because I was our representative in those seats. By this time, our growth and volumes made FFL an attractive addition to the network. Also, prior to this, NETS hired a couple of our top programmers. Perhaps that had something to do with the change of heart...

Meanwhile, our innovation continued in the form of in-store, two-person mini-branches in a number of other grocery stores. While this is common now, FFL was the first in Nebraska to open such facilities. Customers and merchants alike seemed to prefer alternatives to the merchant-operated terminals that didn't involve merchant employees. Plus, we could offer new accounts and even loan applications in these facilities.

So, although supermarkets didn't become S&L branches as initially predicted, our facilities almost made it seem that way.

More importantly, retail checkout terminals were beginning to include interfaces to debit and credit card networks. Merchant-operated terminals in the service areas were no longer a strong business case. Plus, NETS would be able to support these new point-of-sale devices. Also, by then the third generation of ATMs were available, and costs were much more reasonable. So, FFL joined the party, and the terminal network for the world's first electronic transfer system was 'history'.

Sadly, Hinky Dinky stores are no longer a part of the landscape. They were one of the only unionized grocery stores in Nebraska, and the second half of the 70s were not particularly kind to such entities. I remember a big strike that went on for some time, and was probably the last nail in the Hinky Dinky coffin.

And perhaps not surprisingly, NETS is also no longer with us, having been shuttered at the end of 2017. I'm not aware of the details, but I strongly suspect that a larger regional processor destroyed the NETS business case by providing the same services at much lower costs to the financial institutions.

Into the Sunset...

Over the course of the 1970s and 1980s, First Federal Lincoln grew like crazy. From the six branch locations in 1971, FFL reached almost 100 branches in three states. At its peak, the merchant network numbered around 60. Deposits eventually exceeded one billion dollars.

I learned a great deal from this experience: You *can* make a difference and change the world; it requires visionary leadership and unfailing determination; it cannot be done alone—a team of like-minded, passionate, dedicated people will overcome almost any roadblocks; planning is secondary ("Just Do It"); the more people telling you it can't be done is a clear indication you are on the right track.

So, John Dean's vision fueled significant growth, not just in Electronic Funds Transfers. It's impossible to gauge the effect our system has had on the modernization of banking. But, someone had to be first, and today's EFT and debit cards evolved at least in part from our pioneering efforts. I'm humbled to have played a part in this story.

I also learned how corporate strategy can be formulated. In hindsight, I realize that high-level planning isn't something that can be effectively accomplished in one or two day strategic planning sessions. Not that it needs to be daily or weekly, rather, it's best accomplished in an ad hoc manner.

More importantly, information technology representatives need to be a part of strategy formulation. There were ideas—quite a few, actually—that top management wanted to pursue which weren't viable technically in our situation. Had we not been involved, there would have been time wasted at a minimum, and wild goose chases in the form of ill-conceived projects.

I'd like to conclude with a happy ending; unfortunately this will not be the case. First Federal Lincoln is no longer with us. The reason has nothing to do with any of this story. This was not a house of cards that came crashing down. Nor did it have anything to do with the infamous Savings & Loan debacle, which FFL came through relatively unscathed.

It is a story for another time

APPENDIX I - LB269

LEGISLATIVE BILL 269

Approved by the Governor May 2, 1975

Introduced by Murphy, 17

AN ACT to amend section 8-101, Reissue Revised Statutes of Nebraska, 1943, and section 8-157, Revised Statutes Supplement, 1974, relating to banking transactions through the use of manned or unmanned electronic satellite facilities as prescribed; to provide an operative date; and to repeal the original sections.

Be it enacted by the people of the State of Nebraska, Section 1, That section 8-101, Reissue Revised Statutes of Nebraska, 1943, be amended to read as follows:

8-101. As used in sections 8-101 to 8-129, unless the context otherwise requires:

(1) Capital or capital stock shall mean capital stock;

(2) Department shall mean the Department of Banking;

(3) Director shall mean the Director of Banking for the Department of Banking;

(4) Bank or banking corporation shall be construed to mean any incorporated banking institution which shall have been incorporated under the laws of this state as they existed prior to May 9, 1933 and any corporation duly organized under the laws of this state for the purpose of conducting a bank within this state under the provisions of sections 8-101 to 8-129. Bank shall be construed to mean any such banking institution as shall be, in addition to the exercise of other powers, following the practice of repaying deposits upon check, draft, or

order, and of making loans; and

(5) Order shall include orders transmitted by electronic transmission;

(6) Electronic satellite facility shall mean an off-premises unmanned facility or terminal through which banking transactions are transmitted to a bank or banks by means of an electronic impulse;

(7) Manned electronic satellite facility shall mean an off-premises facility, terminal, or place at which banking transactions are brought about with the assistance of one or more persons and transmitted to a bank or banks by means of an electronic impulse. Such person or persons shall not be employees of the bank or banks involved with such transmissions

(8) Making loans shall include advances or credits that are initiated by means of credit card or other transaction card. Transaction card and other transactions, including transactions made pursuant to prior agreements, may be brought about and transmitted by means of an electronic impulse. Such loan transactions including transactions made pursuant to prior agreements shall be subject to sections 8-815 to 8-829, and shall be deemed loans made at the place of business of the bank;

(9) Establishing bank shall mean any bank establishing an electronic satellite facility or a manned electronic satellite facility;

(10) User bank shall mean any bank which desires to avail itself and its customers of an electronic satellite facility or manned electronic satellite facility services;

(11) Bank employees shall include bank holding company and affiliate employees;

(12) Switch shall mean an installation where a transaction impulse is received and the transaction message is immediately routed and electronically transmitted to a processing

center. A switch may be a processing center;

(13) Impulse shall mean an electronic impulse;

(14) A processing center shall mean a place, designated by a user bank, capable of receiving and processing electronic impulse transactions; and

(15) Insolvent shall mean a condition in which (a) the actual cash market value of the assets of a bank is insufficient to pay its liabilities to its depositors, or (b) a bank is unable to meet the demands of its creditors in the usual and customary manner, or (c) a bank, after demand in writing by the Director of Banking, fails to make good any deficiency in its reserves as required by law, or (d) the stockholders of a bank, after written demand by the Director of Banking, fail to make good an impairment of its capital or surplus.

Sec. 2. That section 8-157, Revised Statutes Supplement, 1974, be amended to read as follows:

8-187. (1) No bank shall maintain any branch bank and, except as provided in subsection (2) or subsections (3) to (9) of this section, the general business of every bank shall be transacted at the place of business specified in its charter.

(2) With the approval of the director, (a) any bank may maintain an attached auxiliary teller office, and (b) any bank may establish and maintain not more than two detached auxiliary teller offices, to be used as motor vehicle and walkup off-street banking facilities, such offices to be within the corporate limits of the city in which such bank is located. Any bank that establishes and maintains two auxiliary teller offices shall located one of such offices within three miles of the premises specified as its place of business in its charter. Neither shall be

located within three hundred feet of another nonparticipating bank or within fifty feet of another auxiliary teller office. The services of such auxiliary teller offices whether attached to or detached from the bank shall be limited to receiving deposits of every kind and nature, cashing checks or orders to pay, issuing exchange, and receiving payments payable at the bank.

(3) With the approval of the director, any bank or banks pay establish and maintain any number of electronic satellite facilities or manned electronic satellite facilities at which all banking transactions, defined as receiving deposits of every kind and nature and crediting such to customer accounts, cashing checks and cash withdrawals transfer of funds from checking accounts to savings accounts, transfer of funds from savings accounts to checking accounts, transfer of funds from either checking accounts and savings accounts to accounts of other customers, payment transfers from customer accounts maintained by other bank customers of the bank, including preauthorized draft authority, preauthorized loans and credit transactions, receiving payments payable at the bank or otherwise, and such other transactions that the Director of Banking upon application, notice, and bearing may approve, may be accepted. Such electronic satellite facilities or manned electronic satellite facilities may be established only by a bank as defined in subdivision (9) of section 8-101 or by a national banking association whose main chartered office is located in the State of Nebraska. Neither such electronic satellite facilities, the manned electronic satellite facilities, nor the transactions conducted thereat shall be construed as the establishment of a branch bank or as branch banking. Such facilities shall be available on a nondiscriminating basis for us by customers any other bank becoming a user bank. It shall not be deemed discrimination if a facility does not

The Dawn of Debit Cards

offer the same transaction services as other facilities.

Any bank may become a user bank by agreeing to pay the establishing bank its pro rata transaction and other costs, including a reasonable return on capital expenditures incurred in establishing and maintaining such facilities. The establishing bank shall file with the director the information necessary to originate a transaction at any facility. Such information must contain a means of designating the bank or processor to which such transactions shall be switched, and must also contain information adequate to perform authorization of cash withdrawal and other transactions authorized by this section. The director shall make such information available to any other bank desiring to become a user bank. The establishing bank shall be responsible for transmitting transactions originating from its facility to a switch, but nothing contained in this section my be construed to provide that any in-house or auxiliary teller office premises transactions shall be required to go through a switch. The director shall refuse to approve the establishment of any electronic satellite facilities or manned electronic satellite facilities unless such facilities will be available on a nondiscriminating basis through methods and processes that the establishing bank has provided for switching transactions. Once approval is given fro the facility of an establishing bank, the director, upon notice and after a hearing, may revoke the approval for the facility or may suspend the use of such facility if he determines that it is not available on a nondiscriminating basis, that the necessary information is not on file with the director, or that transactions originated by customers of user banks are not being switched or processing centers. Nothing in this section may be construed to prohibit nonbank employees from assisting in transactions originated at the facilities, and such assistance shall not be deemed to be engaging in the business of banking. Such nonbank employees may be trained in the use of the facilities by bank employees.

(4) An establishing bank shall not be deemed to make a facility available on a nondiscriminating basis if, through personnel services offered, advertising on or off the facility premises, or otherwise, it discriminates in the use of the facility against any user bank.

(5) Off-premises electronic satellite facilities and manned electronic satellite facilities may be established and maintained by a bank or by a group of two or more banks or a combination of a bank or banks and a third party. No one, through personnel services offered, advertising on or off the facility premises, or otherwise, may discriminate in the use of the facility against any other user bank desiring to use the services of the facility.

(6) It is an intent of this section that this that this section shall apply to banks chartered by the State of Nebraska and all national banking associations whose main chartered offices are located in the State of Nebraska and that there be an equal opportunity to all Nebraska banks for the use of and access to a switch and that no discrimination shall exist or preferential treatment be given in either the operation of such switch or the charges for use thereof. The operation of such switch shall be with the approval of the Director of Banking. Approval of such switch shall be given by the Director of Banking when he shall determine that its design and operation are such as to provide access thereto and use thereof by any Nebraska bank without discrimination as to access or cost of its use.

(7) If the director, upon notice and hearing, determines at any time that the design or operation of a switch or provision for use thereof does discriminate against any bank in

providing access thereto and use thereof either through access thereto or by virtue of the cost of its use, he may revoke his approval of such switch operation and forthwith order the discontinuance of the operation of such switch.

(8) If it shall be determined by the Director of Banking, after notice and hearing, that discrimination agains any bank has taken place or that one bank has been preferred over another or that any bank or person has not complied with any of the provisions of this section, he shall forthwith issue a cease and desist order or an order for compliance within ten days from the date of the order and upon noncompliance with such order, the offending bank shall become ineligible to receive and hold any deposits of any nature of the State of Nebraska or any political subdivision thereof.

(9) The provisions of sections 8-101 and 8-157 shall apply to banks and their activities only. Nothing in such sections may be construed to provide any authority for any nonbank institution to engage in any of the banking transactions enumerated in this section. When reference is made in this section to activities by third parties, such activities shall be limited to the ownership, operation, and maintenance of electronic satellite facilities.

(10) Nothing in this section shall prohibit ordinary clearing house transactions between banks.

Sec. 3. This act shall become operative on January 1, 1976.

Sec. 4. That original section 8-101, Reissue Revised Statutes of Nebraska, 1943, and section 8-157, Revised Statutes Supplement, 1974, are repealed.

APPENDIX II - 1975 Nebraska Supreme Court Decision

ST. EX REL. MEYER v. Am. Comm. Stores Corp.

228 N.W.2d 299 (1975)

193 Neb. 634

STATE of Nebraska ex rel. Clarence A. H. MEYER, Attorney General of the State of Nebraska, Appellant, v. AMERICAN COMMUNITY STORES CORPORATION, a Corporation, Appellee, Independent Bakers Association of America, Amicus Curiae.

No. 39747.

\Supreme Court of Nebraska.

May 1, 1975.

*300 Clarence A. H. Meyer, Atty. Gen., Ralph H. Gillan, Asst. Atty. Gen., Lincoln, for appellant.

Delehant, Croker & Huck, Omaha, for appellee.

Thomas C. Brickle, Richard W. Peterson, Washington, D. C., for amicus curiae.

Heard before McCOWN and NEWTON, JJ., COLWELL and CLARK, District Judges, and KUNS, Retired District Judge.

McCOWN, Justice.

This is a quo warranto action brought by the State of Nebraska through its Attorney General against American Community Stores Corporation. The action seeks forfeiture of the corporate charter, rights, and privileges of the respondent on the ground that the respondent had engaged in the banking or savings and loan business without authorization, in violation of the laws of the state. The District Court for Lancaster County found that the respondent was not engaged in the banking or savings and loan business and dismissed the information. The State has appealed.

The respondent, American Community Stores Corporation, is a Texas corporation licensed to do business in Nebraska. It operates 35 supermarket stores in the state under the name of "Hinky Dinky." The annual food sales volume is in excess of $100 million. To increase food sales, respondent has traditionally offered incidental services to its customers, including the cashing of checks, selling of stamps, selling of money orders, free use of telephones, and the availability of postal boxes.

*301 First Federal Savings and Loan Association of Lincoln is a federally chartered savings and loan association subject to the jurisdiction of the Federal Home Loan Bank Board. On January 9, 1974, the Federal Home Loan Bank Board authorized First Federal to install computer terminals in two of the Hinky Dinky stores in Lincoln. On January 14, 1974, the computer terminals owned by First Federal were installed in the two stores. First Federal paid no consideration to respondent, nor does respondent pay First Federal any fees or compensation. Neither is any charge made to the customer for the service, which is called TMS (transmatic money service). The Federal Home Land Bank Board refers to the system as a "place-of-business funds transfer system."

The TMS service is a means by which a TMS depositor of First Federal of Lincoln can communicate with First Federal in order to make deposits and withdrawals by means of a computer terminal installed at a location such as one of the respondent's stores. A customer in the Hinky Dinky store cannot open a First Federal account, nor deposit or withdraw from a passbook or

The Dawn of Debit Cards

certificate account with First Federal, nor make a loan payment. The computer terminal itself is about the size of an adding machine and is connected by a regular telephone to the computer at the home office of First Federal in Lincoln. The terminal is located at the courtesy counter in respondent's store. The respondent maintains an interest-bearing transmatic savings account with First Federal, initially $25,000, which is replenished from time to time as needed. Each depositor of First Federal who uses the system must have a transmatic savings account at First Federal and both the store and the customer have a transmatic card which must be used with each transaction. Transactions are handled exclusively by respondent's employees.

If a customer wishes to deposit in his or her First Federal account, the customer goes to the courtesy counter of the store and obtains a transaction slip from a store employee. When that slip is filled out, the respondent's employee then places the two electronically embossed and coded TMS cards in the terminal. One card identifies the store and the other identifies the customer. The customer also has to furnish certain personal confidential numbers, which are not contained on the card, for the purpose of verifying that the person using the card is authorized to use it. The store employee then uses the telephone on the terminal to activate the on-line computer, which is located at the main office of First Federal. The computer then verifies the account and the information. Once verification has been made, the transaction proceeds instantaneously. The computer debits the store's account at First Federal in the amount of the customer's deposit; credits the customer's account at First Federal in the same amount; and notifies the terminal operator that the transaction has been completed. The store then accepts from the customer the money or check representing the deposit and the money is placed in the cash register with other money of the store.

In the case of a withdrawal the procedure is essentially the same except that in this case the computer debits the customer's First Federal account and credits the store's First Federal account, and the store then pays the amount of the withdrawal in cash to the customer from the store's cash drawer.

The TMS operation at respondent's two stores in Lincoln began experimentally on January 14, 1974, and continued until March 1, 1974. It was then temporarily suspended and later begun again. During the experimental period from January 14 to March 1, 1974, 3,169 individual transactions were initiated from the two stores, involving a total deposit volume of $333,085.80, and a total withdrawal volume of $40,605.70, an average of $117.92 per transaction.

The evidence also establishes that state chartered savings and loan associations *302 maintain agents in cities or areas where they have no home office or branch. These agents accept deposits and transmit them to the home office and make on-the-spot withdrawals or transmit withdrawal requests to the home office. They also solicit business and handle other activities for the home office. The Assistant Director of Banking of the State of Nebraska, who is the supervisor of state chartered savings and loan associations for the department, testified that there is nothing in the statutes to cover this activity by agents of savings and loan associations, and that so far as he knows, there is nothing that would prohibit anyone from acting as agent for a savings and loan association in such transactions. He conceded that the respondent could act as an agent for a state chartered savings and loan association in Nebraska under current state statutes.

The State contends that performance of the activities above described by the respondent through the means of a computer terminal located in its store constitutes engaging in a banking or savings and loan business. The evidence, however, is conclusive that the operations challenged here have been specifically authorized by the Federal Home Loan Bank Board, which has jurisdiction over the operations of First Federal Savings and Loan Association; and also that the actions of respondent were not in violation of any statute of this state governing the carrying on of a savings and loan business. The State's position therefore rests on the assertion that the actions of the respondent here constitute engaging in a banking business.

The State contends that respondent's actions violate section 8-114, R.R.S.1943, and, in particular, the language of that section which provides: "It shall be unlawful for any corporation to receive money upon deposit or conduct a bank under the laws of this state, until such corporation shall have complied with all the provisions and requirements of sections 8-101 to 8-1,122." The State argues that the respondent is itself receiving deposits and paying withdrawals, and that this amounts to carrying on the business of banking as well as being in violation of statutory provisions limiting branch banking.

This court has continuously held that the relationship of banker and depositor can only be created by contract, express or implied. In City of Lincoln v. First Nat. Bank, 146 Neb. 221, 19 N.W.2d 156, this court said: "`The term "deposit," when used in connection with a banking transaction, denotes a contractual relationship ensuing from the delivery, by one known as the "depositor," of moneys, funds, or things into the possession of the bank, which receives the same upon the agreement to pay, repay, or return, upon the order or demand of the depositor, the moneys, funds, or equivalent amount, or things, received; * * *.'"

The general rule is that a bank which receives a general deposit of money becomes the debtor of the depositor. Glass v. Nebraska State Bank, 175 Neb. 673, 122 N.W.2d 882. The undisputed evidence here establishes that the element of a debtor and creditor relationship essential to any

Jim Beitel

bank deposit or withdrawal of funds never exists between the store and the customer. The customer is transacting business with First Federal through the use of a computer terminal in the store, and the actions of the store facilitate that transaction. The State wishes to disregard not only the facts of electronic technology but the undisputed evidence in this case. The computer terminal is analogous to communication equipment of other kinds in that it simply transmits information to the central computer of First Federal. The deposit and withdrawal transactions are electronically effected and perfected by the computer on the records and premises of First Federal. At no time does First Federal have possession or ownership of any cash or funds physically transferred on the store premises between the store and the customer. It seems clear to us that under the operations outlined here, the First Federal depositor is giving funds *303 to or receiving funds from the respondent's store, and the store is simply a financial as well as an operational intermediary between the depositor and First Federal.

We are advised that this case is one of first impression in the courts. Various federal agencies having jurisdiction over financial institutions have determined that computer terminals located in stores or other places of business, and manned by an employee of the store, may be established under specified conditions by a financial institution under their jurisdiction. Such operations do not constitute an illegal banking or savings and loan operation by the store, nor the carrying on of business at an unauthorized branch by the financial institution involved. See, Federal Home Loan Bank Board Document 74-573, 39 Fed.Reg. 23991, and Resolution 74-575, June 26, 1974; Comptroller of the Currency, Department of the Treasury, 39 Fed.Reg. 44416, December 24, 1974; National Credit Union Administration, 39 Fed.Reg. 30107, August 21, 1974. See, also, Opinion No. 74-196 Attorney General of Kansas, June 12, 1974. We have found no ruling by any regulatory agency to the contrary.

The State has the burden of proving that the actions of the respondent constitute the carrying on of a banking or savings and loan business. The evidence is uncontradicted, however, that the respondent does not accept or retain deposits, nor promise to repay them or return them to anyone. The respondent's activities are restricted to acting as an intermediary and assisting in the transfer of funds between First Federal and First Federal's depositors. The State has failed to cite authority in direct support of its legal position, and has failed to sustain the burden of proof on the facts.

Where a federal savings and loan association installs a computer terminal in a retail store as authorized by the Federal Home Loan Bank Board for the purpose of facilitating the electronic transfer of funds between the association and its depositors, the owner or operator of the store, by manning the computer terminal and assisting in such electronic transfer of funds under the facts here, is not engaging in either a banking or savings and loan business.

The judgment of the District Court was correct and is affirmed.

Affirmed.

About the Author

Jim Beitel is an Information Technology management coach/consultant with 40+ years of experience in IT management and practice: He's provided assistance to well-known financial service companies and with FFL, held positions from part-time night computer operator to Executive Vice President/Director of Information Services, and everything in between.

He currently resides in Lincoln, Nebraska with his wife, Sue (who also contributed to the successes of both FFL and TMS Corp.), a dog and a pond full of goldfish. Jim ranks ahead of the goldfish. Barely.

Please feel free to let Jim know of any problems, concerns, questions or comments at: jbeitel@jbeitel.com.

www.ingramcontent.com/pod-product-compliance
Lightning Source LLC
Chambersburg PA
CBHW071126240526
45465CB00024B/1404